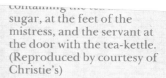

ing. Before then the British tea ceremony was most solemnly performed when the ladies retired after dinner to take tea in the drawing-room. The men remained in the dining-room and drank heavily before going to join them. Tea-drinking quickly became a national habit, and required little excuse at any time. The Regency socialite Captain Gronow recounted the following incident in his memoirs:

> General Lincoln Stanhope once told me, that after an absence of several years in India, he made his reappearance at Harrington House, and found the family, as he had left them on his departure, drinking tea in the long gallery. On his presenting himself, his father's only observation and speech of welcome to him was 'Hallo Linky, my dear boy! delighted to see you. Have a cup of tea?'

❧ Too Good for the Common People?

Because tea was expensive in the 18th century, the drink was often made by the mistress in the drawing-room rather than by a servant in the kitchen. If the servant could not steal the mistress's tea, it was often worth re-using her old tealeaves. Jonathan Swift explained in his satirical *Directions to Servants* in 1745 that there was now an 'execrable custom got among Ladies . . . the invention of small Chests and Trunks, with Lock and Key, wherein they keep the Tea and Sugar, without which it is impossible for a Waiting-maid to live. For, by this means you are forced to buy brown Sugar, and pour Water upon the Leaves, when they have lost all their Spirit and Taste.' A typical locking chest of this kind contains two tea jars and a covered sugar bowl, all of silver (pl 2). Because the mistress made the tea in the drawing-room in front of her guests, even the tea-kettle was often of silver. It had a lamp underneath to keep the water hot, so that it could remain on hand for refilling the teapot.

The high cost of tea meant also that most early teapots were small. Really large pots which look like teapots were often used in the 18th century for punch. The main reason for the high cost of tea was that it was heavily taxed by Government. To avoid the tax, a great deal of tea was smuggled in from the Continent. Parson Woodforde wrote in his diary for 29 March 1777: 'Andrews the Smuggler brought me this night about 11 o'clock a bag of Hyson tea 6 pound weight. He frightened us a little by whistling under the parlour window just as we were going to bed. I gave him some Genever [gin] and paid him for the tea at 10s 6d per pound.' A workman might then have earned about 10s 6d a week, and Andrews' price did not include the tea tax! When the working classes took up drinking tea, their 'betters' were shocked. Jonas Hanway, in his 'Essay on Tea' in 1757, exclaimed:

> To what a height of folly must a nation be arrived, when the common people are not satisfied with wholesome food at home, but must go to the remotest regions to please a vicious palate! There is a certain lane near Richmond where beggars are often seen, in the summer season, drinking their tea. You may see labourers who are mending the roads drinking their tea; it is even drank in cinder-carts . . .

The poor had to make do with adulterated varieties of tea containing hawthorn leaves dyed with chemicals which were sometimes poisonous. In 1784 high grain prices were putting ale, the staple drink of the poor, out of their reach. The tea merchants, led by Richard Twining, persuaded the Government to reduce drastically the tax on tea, admitting that 'tea has become an economical substitute to the middle and lower classes of society for malt liquor, the price of which renders it impossible for them to procure the quantity sufficient for them as their only drink.' Water was, of course, not usually safe to drink unless it had been fermented into ale or boiled.

Cheaper tea after 1784 meant that larger teapots were made, and in 1839 the British began to drink tea grown in their own dominions in India. Tea has remained ever since as our distinctive national drink, and teapots can be seen as the most typically British type of pot. Can there be a pottery or porcelain factory in

3 The dangers of not knowing the etiquette of the teaspoon, 1825. (Reproduced by courtesy of Twinings)

A Tea Party — or English Manners — and French Politeness.

A Frenchman not aware of the custom, constantly returned his Cup without the spoon in it — which being immediately replenished by the Lady of the house, he thought it a point of politeness to drink the contents which he continued to do, to the great surprise of the company until he perceived the Lady pouring out the 14th Cup, when he rose in great agony and cried Ah! Madame, excuse me I can take no more.

the country which has not made them? The teapot has been a key product for most factories, and has been redesigned more frequently and more carefully than any other item. Between 1790 and 1840 the fashionable shape for teapots changed with astonishing rapidity. When Jane Austen's heroine came down for breakfast at Northanger Abbey and admired her host's teaset, he apologised that it was two years old and already out of date.

Tea-drinking held an important place in Georgian social life. It embodied people's desire to live in a stylish, refined – they would have said 'genteel' – way. The teapot's importance as a fashionable item of consumer goods explains why such inventiveness was lavished on its design. To find a modern comparision one would have to look at the latest in electronic home entertainment and kitchen gadgets. The refined Georgian lifestyle included the etiquette of returning your teacup with the spoon in it if you did not want a refill. A cartoon (pl 3) shows a hapless Frenchman who does not know the rule, has kept on drinking out of politeness, and is about to burst.

The teapot's place at the centre of social life made it a popular vehicle for messages of all kinds. Some pots carry pious sentiments, celebrate Wellington's victories in the Peninsular War, or bear political propaganda, like the pot simply inscribed 'Wilkes and Liberty', 'No.45'. John Wilkes was a radical politician who, in issue 45 of the magazine *The North Briton* published an attack on the king. When he stood as a candidate for Middlesex in the election of 1768, there were riots, and '45' became the slogan of the day. The Spanish ambassador was dragged from his carriage, turned upside down and had '45' scrawled on the soles of his shoes. Other pots carry a timeless message, like the print of the Miller's Maid grinding old men young again, or the cheerfully mis-spelt 'love and live Happay' (pl 4).

4 Pearlware painted in underglaze colours, about 1800

Early British Teapots

The imported Chinese pots provided British potters with the original stimulus to create delicate teawares. They did not succeed in making porcelain on a commercial scale until 1745, but were already learning to rival the imports by using materials and techniques of their own. Rather like the alchemists who were trying to make gold and precious stones by artificial means, the potters invented new types of ware to which they gave names like 'agate' (pl 5), 'jasper' (pl 13) and 'tortoiseshell', or which they compared to rubies and shiny black basalt stone.

In the first half of the 18th century, the established pottery area of north Staffordshire had no tradition of painting with a brush, but used different coloured clays and glazes for decoration. Faced with the Chinese challenge, the potters began in the 1730s and '40s to work clays of different colours together in strips to create banded or marbled effects (pl 5). This was an incredibly laborious way to create a pattern on a teapot, and shows how far potters would go to avoid picking up a brush! An easier method was to apply clay flowers or figures of one colour on to pots of another colour, as the Chinese did on some of their fine red wares. Alternatively powdered glazes of different colours could be used to achieve a variegated or dappled finish. Josiah Wedgwood's first commercial success in the late 1750s was a green glaze suitable for decorating pots in the form of fruit and vegetables, which were the current fashion (pl 7).

Cauliflower teapots and other fancy shapes could not be 'thrown' on the potter's wheel, but were made in plaster moulds. House and camel teapots were being made in this way as early as 1740 (pl 6), but the basic 'thrown' globular teapot remained the most popular shape until the 1780s.

The Mystery of Porcelain

By 1745 Chelsea was producing the first successful English porcelain, and other china factories sprang up in rapid succession. This first generation of English porcelains was made of quite different materials from the Oriental or German (Meissen) porcelain which they hoped to rival. The latter was made of china clay and china stone, fired to a very high temperature, and is known as hard-paste porcelain. The English did not know the secret of its manufacture, and their porcelains, fired to a lower temperature, are known as soft-pastes.

5 Agate ware, about 1740

7 A cauliflower pot,
creamware with green
glaze, about 1760–70

Some porcelain recipes were better than others. The Bow factory in the eastern suburbs of London added bone-ash to the mix to give the wares extra strength. Worcester included soapstone, which made the china more resistant to heat (pl 8). A consumer guide in the *Gentleman's Magazine* in 1763 compared those English porcelains, which were cheaper than the Chinese, and reported: 'except Worcester they all wear brown and are subject to crack, especially the glazing, by boiling water.' A shop in Leeds selling English china in 1760 offered to replace teapots 'if broke with hot water'. As late as the 1780s the Derby factory was still having problems with its teapots 'flying', that is, flying to pieces.

No wonder that people wanted Oriental porcelain if they could get it. The fashionable Chinese-style decoration of much early English porcelain must often have helped the home-grown product to pass off as Chinese. The Bow factory advertised itself as 'New Canton' and Worcester started life as 'the Worcester Tonquin Manufacture'.

Most factories depended for survival on the production of teawares decorated in blue before glazing. They were competing with Chinese blue and white porcelain, which was imported in vast quantities. Blue, made from cobalt, was the only colour which could be trusted to withstand the temperature at which the glaze was fired. If other colours were wanted, they had to be added after the glaze was fired. Further firings at lower temperatures were then needed to fuse the colours on to the glazed surface. This usually made the pots at least twice the price of blue and white ones.

Worcester and Bow pioneered the use of printed decoration in the 1750s. At first printing was seen as superior to much painting in terms of precision and quality control. The delicate early prints were applied after glazing, so the pots cost more than painted blue and white ones. By 1760, however, Worcester was printing in blue before glazing, and soon printing was seen mainly as a cheap substitute for painting. High quality printing over the glaze did make a come-back, however, between 1790 and 1820, in the form of stipple prints resembling the book illustrations of the period, from which they were often copied.

8 Worcester porcelain, about 1755–8

🍵 Industrial Revolution

Ten tons of coal were required to fire one ton of clay in a pottery kiln. Firing to a lower temperature used less coal. Earthenware was therefore cheaper to make than the higher-fired stoneware pottery or porcelains. High kiln temperatures were also difficult to achieve, because there was not yet any accurate means of measuring them. About 1760 Wedgwood produced the first commercially successful earthenware which was pale enough to look something like porcelain (pl 9). It is nowadays called creamware, and has been called Britain's greatest contribution in the history of ceramics. By 1780 it had captured the market, not only in Britain but throughout Europe and in North America. It could be painted or printed like porcelain, but generally after glazing, for the glaze would give underglaze blue a green or yellowish tinge.

By 1780 a version with a blue tinge to the glaze made the pots look even more like porcelain and enabled blue decoration to be done before glazing. Most potters called the new ware 'china glaze', though it is now usually known as pearlware. It was the beginning of the blue-printed white pottery which dominated the market between 1800 and 1850.

A Plymouth chemist, William Cookworthy, discovered in Cornwall the ingredients – china clay and china stone – which enabled him to make hard-paste porcelain like the Chinese. The glaze was fired at a much higher temperature than for soft-paste porcelain, and this caused problems, especially with underglaze blue. By 1781 the factory he founded at Bristol had closed, and the patent rights in his invention were sold to a group of Staffordshire potters, who set up a factory at New Hall. They made English hard-paste porcelain a success by firing to a high temperature before the ware was glazed, and using a glaze that would fire at lower temperature (pl 10). This was the way in which soft-paste porcelains were fired.

Factory producing the new type of porcelain proliferated even before New Hall's patent ran out in 1796 (pl 11). The writing was on the wall for soft-paste porcelain, which was not as durable. By 1800 the new factories of Spode and Minton (pl 14) were adding bone-ash to china clay and china stone to make a creamy white body, bone china. This became the standard English porcelain body throughout the 19th century and remains very popular today.

10 New Hall porcelain, about 1785–90

11 Chamberlain's Worcester porcelain, about 1800

❦ Sheffield and Ancient Rome

The shapes of pottery were always liable to be influenced by their more expensive counterparts in silver. In the years around 1770 a revolution took place in the silver trade. For the first time it had become possible to make vessels of base metal covered with a thin layer of silver. This fused plate, nowadays known as Sheffield plate, could only be made in sheets, but was very much cheaper than solid silver. In order to compete, the silver trade had to cut its prices by reducing the weight of precious metal in each item. Teapots began to be made of thin sheets of silver.

By one of those coincidences of history, this was just the time when changes in the art-world were beginning to make globular teapots look unfashionable. The publication of archaeological discoveries at Pompeii and Herculaneum had revealed to excited Georgian eyes the interior decoration of the Romans, and architects like Robert Adam were cleverly adapting the style for everything from palaces down to knife-boxes. This design movement is nowadays known as neoclassicism. There was a ready market for decorative objects that would suit fashionable rooms of this kind. Just because the Greeks and Romans had not had teapots, this did not prevent designers from coming up with modern classical ones (pl 13). The globular shape must have looked not at all classical and rather dumpy.

The metalworkers found that teapots shaped like boxes, with curved or angled corners, were much easier to make out of sheet metal than the old globular teapots. The potters imitated these shapes (pls 10–14). Since they were not circular in plan, they could not be 'thrown' on the wheel, but had to be made in plaster moulds. The age when potteries were full of 'throwers' was coming to an end, and their places would be taken by workmen using moulds. When the round teapot returned to fashion around 1820 (pl 15), it too would be made in moulds rather than thrown.

The ideal material for teapots in the spirit of the vases and urns of ancient Rome was pottery with little or no glaze covering it. This would show the fine detail of moulded or applied reliefs without hiding it under a thick layer of glaze. The hard pottery called stoneware was dense enough to be impervious to liquids even without a glaze. Wedgwood changed the style of his red stoneware pots from 'Chinese' to Roman with a new brand name, 'rosso antico' (ancient red). Stoneware in other colours was developed, including the famous jasperware for which Wedgwood is chiefly remembered (pl 13), cane-coloured ware and white ware. The most popular colour was usually called 'Egyptian black', though Wedgwood called his 'basaltes'. He reckoned this black was popular for teapots because it showed off the desirable whiteness of a hostess's hands!

12 Pearlware, about 1800. The circular scene is printed, the rest of the decoration painted

13 Adams jasper ware,
about 1790

14 Minton porcelain,
1812–16

15 Davenport porcelain,
about 1825

❦ The Fashionable Shape

After about 1790 a new shape of teapot was introduced in porcelain every few years, and most porcelain factories would make the new shape in order to keep up with their competitors. The first 'box' shape, a lozenge plan with straight sides (pl 10), was quickly followed by an oval plan with curved sides (pl 11). Later shapes are now known by the names given them in a Shape Book of 1820 made for use in the Spode factory. The 'Old Oval' has straight sides and was introduced about 1795 (pl 12). The 'New Oval', introduced about 1805, has curved sides and a cover which sits down inside a raised rim. The 'London' shape, introduced about 1812, has a projecting shoulder and an oblong plan with rounded-off corners (pl 14).

In the 1820s the influence of the Romantic Movement began to affect all aspects of interior design. There was a reaction against the restrained shapes of neoclassicism. A low version of the round teapot had already come back into fashion (pl 15), and soon it began to erupt into swaggering curves. By 1830 pots were giving themselves airs on feet and pedestals, while spouts and handles became scrolling gestures (pl 16). A staggering variety of flamboyant shapes was made, almost entirely in bone china or white earthenware, which looked very like it.

❦ Fun and Function

By the time of the Great Exhibition in 1851, critical reaction had again set in. A teapot which sat expressively gesturing on the table began to look out of place, its gestures insincere. Henry Cole, the leading light behind the Great Exhibition, had designed a plain teapot, enlivened only by a lion-mask spout, to show people what they ought to want. The age of 'designer good taste' setting itself up against what it saw as 'popular bad taste', had arrived.

In the late 19th century novelty teapots in wacky shapes were made (pl 17). The trend has continued, with big upsurges in the 1930s (pl 18) and again since 1970. All three periods have been marked by heavy emphasis on 'designer good taste', and it is tempting to suggest that teapots in the shape of fish or Simple Simon have been a sort of 'safety valve', an escape from serious design and a chance to let one's hair down. The earnestness about 'form and function' which has dogged design in Britain since 1851 has itself led to some strange designs for teapots. Mr J. Royle's patent self-pourer of 1886 works by air pressure (pl 19). The metal cover has a deep flange, and when pressed down it makes exactly a cupful of tea pour out of the spout. Lord Dundonald's 'SYP' (Simple Yet Perfect) design of 1905 prevents the tea from stewing (pl 20). The tealeaves

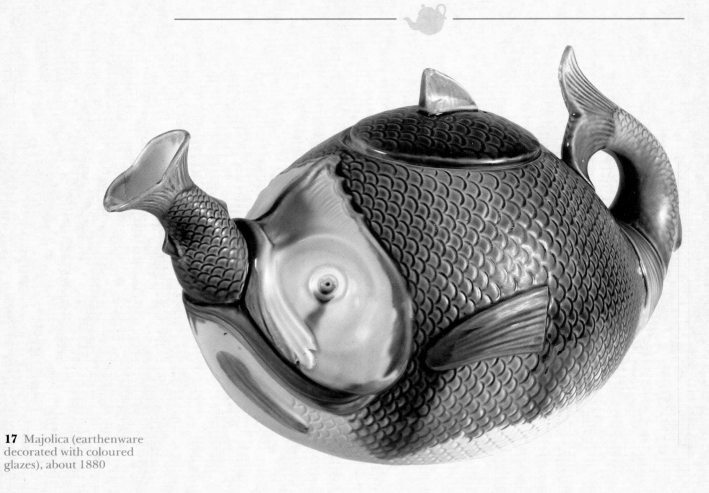

17 Majolica (earthenware decorated with coloured glazes), about 1880

18 'Simple Simon' earthenware, about 1930–40